Magical Puzzles

Fairy Puzzles

Written by
Samantha Williams

Illustrated by
Samantha Loman

WINDMILL BOOKS

Published in 2020 by **Windmill Books**, an imprint of Rosen Publishing
29 East 21st Street, New York, NY 10010

Illustrated by Samantha Loman
Written by Samantha Williams
Edited by Susannah Bailey
Designed by Well Nice Ltd

Cataloging-in-Publication Data

Names: Williams, Samantha. | Loman, Sam.
Title: Fairy puzzles / Samantha Williams, illustrated by Sam Loman.
Description: New York : Windmill Books, 2020. | Series: Magical puzzles
Identifiers: ISBN 9781538391761 (pbk.) | ISBN 9781538391785 (library bound) | ISBN 9781538391778 (6 pack)
Subjects: LCSH: Picture puzzles--Juvenile literature. | Fairies--Juvenile literature.
Classification: LCC GV1507.P47 W55 2020 | DDC 793.73--dc23

Manufactured in the United States of America

CPSIA Compliance Information: Batch #BS19WM:
For Further Information contact Rosen Publishing, New York, New York at 1-800-237-9932

Contents

Come On In!

Welcome to this magical land, where unicorns roam, fairies fly high, and mermaids splash in a pink lemonade sea. But which pathway leads to the castle? Is it A, B, or C?

Best Fairy Friends

Which fairy doesn't have a BFF
in a matching outfit?

Shiny Crown

Milly the unicorn will crown one of these fairies queen for the day, but which one? Solve the clues to find out.

1. Her hair is braided.

2. She has a heart-shaped wand.

3. She is not wearing ballet shoes.

4. She isn't wearing a belt.

Cloud Kingdom

Can you discover eight differences between these two floating fairy castles?

Find the Fairy

The fairies are playing hide-and-seek with the unicorns
and have hidden among the flowers.
Can you spot all 10 of them?

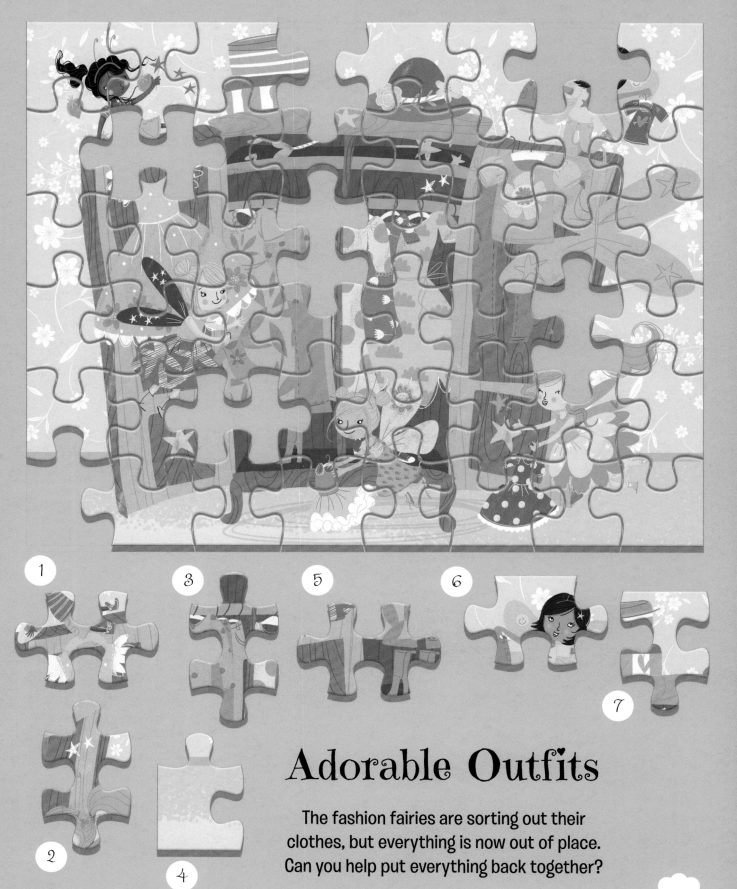

Adorable Outfits

The fashion fairies are sorting out their clothes, but everything is now out of place. Can you help put everything back together?

Code Queen

Ruby has left a coded message for Sparkle. Can you figure out what it says?

_____   _____   _____   _____

_____   _____   _____   _____

BRING	TO	SEA	CUPCAKES
LATER	BEACH	THE	THANKS

HELLO	PLEASE	FLOWER	PARTY

Butterfly Hunt

Eloise and her fairy friends are searching for the special blue butterfly with four wings. Can you help them find it?

Time for Tea!

The furry pet friends are having a picnic.
Can you complete the scene by filling in
the missing pieces?

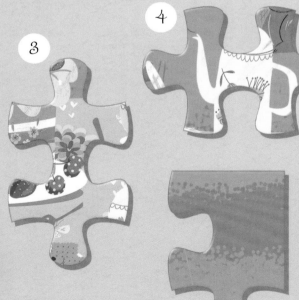

Queen of the Arts

The Fairy Queen loves being creative.
She has painted six unicorn pictures that look identical.
Can you tell which is the odd one out?

Flying Fair

There's a summer fair at the magical castle!
Look at it for two minutes, then turn the page.

Flying Fair

How much can you remember?
Answer these questions on a
separate piece of paper.

1. What is one of the fairies
giving one of the unicorns?

....

2. Which ride is at the
back of the fair?

....

3. Does the fairy looking in the
mirror have blue or pink hair?

....

4. Is the fairy on the merry-go-round
wearing a pink or purple dress?

....

5. Are the flags on the castle
turrets red or yellow?

....

6. What instrument is one
of the fairies playing?

....

Fantasy Fairy Name

Your birth month + your fave sweet treat = your fairy name! For example, if you were born in May and like strawberries, your name would be Violet Moon. Write down yours in your notebook!

JANUARY	POPPY	JULY	SILVER
FEBRUARY	WILLOW	AUGUST	SUGAR
MARCH	BLOSSOM	SEPTEMBER	BLUEBELL
APRIL	STAR	OCTOBER	HONEY
MAY	VIOLET	NOVEMBER	HARVEST
JUNE	IVY	DECEMBER	LILAC

CAKE	DAWN
COOKIES	BREEZE
STRAWBERRIES	MOON
ICE CREAM	GLOW
CHOCOLATE	SHINE
CANDY	SONG
POPCORN	GLIMMER
MILKSHAKE	DEWDROP

My fairy name is:

....

My friend's fairy name is:

....

17

Flowery Trail

The Fairy Queen is lost in the garden! Can you help her find a way across? She has to step on the flowers in a set order. She can go up, down, left, and right, but not diagonally.

1

2

3

Start

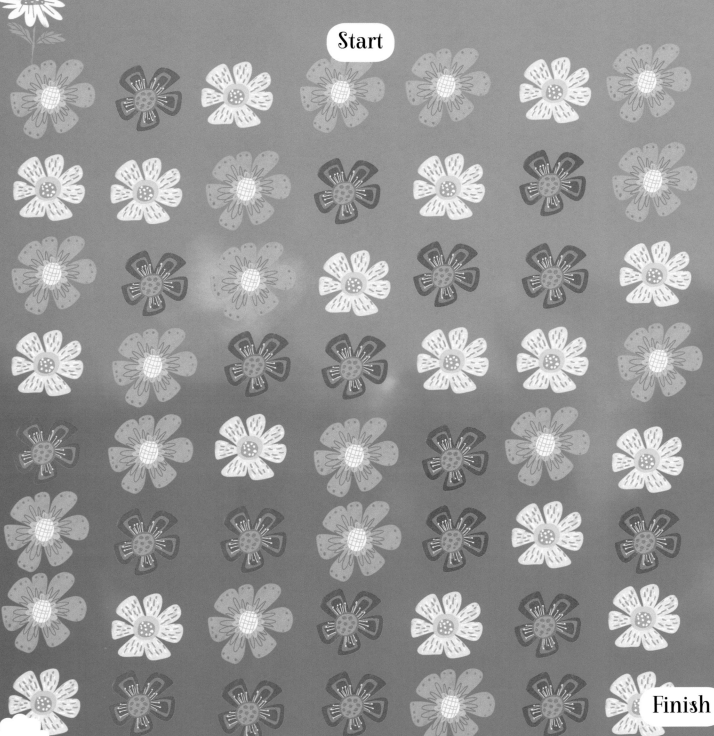

Finish

Gorgeous Garlands

Primrose needs to pick the flower collection with the highest number of sparkle points, so she can make a special garland for her fairy friend, Lily. Which one should she choose?

Tasty Treats!

There's a bake sale, and the fairies have made cakes and cookies. Can you find eight differences between these two yummy scenes?

Magical Mountain

The sugar fairies are flying over the swirly ice cream mountains.
Can you figure out which one hasn't made the journey?

Sprinkle

Flossy

Buttercup

Lollipop

Caramel

Cherry

Sherbet

Sparkling Snow

Snow has fallen! Can you spot all of these objects in this wintry scene?

5 PAIRS OF PINK EARMUFFS

4 GREEN SCARVES

4 BLUE HATS

2 PINK HATS

In the Treetops

The fairies are in the orchard collecting fruit.
Solve the equations to see which basket contains the most!

2

$14 + 8$

1

$36 - 7$

3

$16 + 9$

4

4×6

Dainty Dewdrops

The raindrop fairies are off to collect water from the dew waterfall. Can you guide them through the tropical forest to reach it?

Start

Finish

Delicious Desserts

Look at this picture of the fairy kitchen for two minutes.
Then turn the page, and answer the questions without looking back.

Delicious Desserts

Write your answers on a separate piece of paper.

1. What is the fairy bringing out of the oven?

....

2. Is the yellow fairy wearing a crown or a rose?

....

3. Is the unicorn's apron blue or pink?

....

4. Does the tablecloth have hearts or stars on it?

....

5. How many cups are on the table?

....

6. Which fruit are the fairies using to decorate the cake?

....

Snug Knitwear

It's getting chilly, so the fairies have been making hats and scarves for the unicorns. However, the sparkle threads are in a tangle. Can you figure out which fairy has knitted which item?

Answers

Page 4: Come On In!
Pathway B leads to the castle.

Page 5: Best Fairy Friends

Page 6: Shiny Crown

Page 7: Cloud Kingdom

Page 8: Find the Fairy

Page 9: Adorable Outfits

Page 10: Code Queen
The message is:
Please bring cupcakes to the beach party later.

Page 11: Butterfly Hunt

Page 12: Time for Tea!

Page 13: Queen of the Arts

Page 14: Flying Fair

1 A medal.
2 The ferris wheel.
3 She has pink hair.
4 She is wearing a purple dress.
5 The flags are yellow.
6 The fairy is playing a harp.

Page 18: Flowery Trail

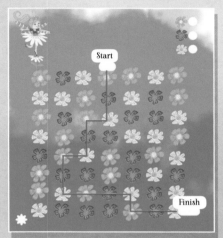

Page 19:
Gorgeous Garlands

Pile A has the most.

A has 19.
B has 11.
C has 17.
D has 18.

Page 20: Tasty Treats

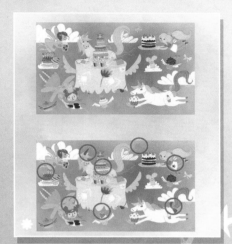

Page 21:
Magical Mountain

Cherry hasn't made the journey.

Page 22: Sparkling Snow

Page 24: In the Treetops

Page 25: Dainty Dewdrops

Page 26:
Delicious Desserts

1 Cookies.
2 The yellow fairy is wearing a crown.
3 The unicorn's apron is blue.
4 Stars.
5 There are three cups on the table.
6 Strawberries.

Page 29: Snug Knitwear

1 D
2 C
3 A
4 B